Vital Xposure

Bush Theatre

I0802457

...blackbird hour

by babirye bukilwa

...blackbird hour was produced by Vital Xposure in association with the Bush Theatre and premiered at the Bush Theatre, London, on 30 January 2025.

...blackbird hour

by babirye bukilwa

Cast

Sissy	Danielle Kassaraté
Eshe	Evlyne Oyedokun
Michael	Ivan Oyik
Ella	Olivia Nakintu

Creative Team

Director	malakaï sargeant
Designer	Khadija Raza
Lighting Designer	Jahmiko Marshall
Sound Designer & Composer	Mwen
Creative Captions & Video Designer	Will Monks
Intimacy Director & Movement Director	Asha Jennings-Grant
Producer	Vital Xposure

Production Crew

Production Manager	Crin Claxon
Company Stage Manager	Danielle Adéyínká-Uche
Technical Stage Manager	Joe Colgan
Stage Manager	Alison Pottinger

Access Team

Access Coordinator	Pia Richards-Glöckner
Integrated Audio Description Consultant	Margo Cargill
Audio Description Writer	Michael Achtman
Creative Captions Consultant	Jean St Clair

Marketing Team

Marketing Associates	Cup of Ambition
Audience Development Associate	Bid Mosaku
Artwork Designer	Kieron Lewis

Vital Xposure Team

Artistic Lead	Stephen Bailey
Executive Director	Theresa Veith
General Manager	Foteini Galanopoulou
Productions Assistant	Ella Kennedy

Cast

Danielle Kassaraté | Sissy

Danielle's credits include: *The Architect* (Greenwich Docklands Festival/ATC); *I Wonder If* (Young Vic); *Till Death Do Us Part* (Theatre 503); *...cake* (Theatre Peckham); *The Curious Incident of The Dog in the Night-Time* (Gielgud/International Tour); *The Color Purple* (Birmingham Hippodrome/Leicester Curve); *Macbeth* (Queen's Hornchurch); *Wildfire* (Hampstead).

Evlyne Oyedokun | Eshe

Evlyne is an African Caribbean Autistic Actress who graduated from RADA in 2016. Her theatre credits include: *Autistic as Fuck* (Barbican); *Cinderella* (Northern Stage); *An Inspector Calls* (UK world tour); *One Under* (Graeae).

Her film and TV credits include *RIPD2* (Netflix 2022) and *Kirkmoore* (BBC3).

Ivan Oyik | Michael

His recent credits include: *by their fruits* (Initiative.dkf/Theatre503) and *Ludwig* (BBC One). Ivan's first professional opportunity was *Blue/Orange* directed by Daniel Bailey for which he was nominated for The Stage Debut Award.

Other credits include *Shook* (Southwark Playhouse); *Red Pitch* (Ovalhouse) and a three episode story arc in *Doctors* (BBC).

Olivia Nakintu | Ella

Olivia attended London Academy of Music & Dramatic Art.

Her credits include: the role of Zadie in the short film *Mango* directed by Joan Iyiola; 'Esther' in *Better*, 'Jay' in *Am I Being Unreasonable* (BBC) and Amber in *Vera* (ITV).

Creative Team

babirye bukilwa | Writer

babirye bukilwa is an actor and writer for stage, audio, and screen.

Their first play, *...blackbird hour*, was shortlisted for the Bruntwood Prize for Playwriting in 2019, the inaugural Women's Prize for Playwriting 2020, and the Alfred Fagon Award 2020. The play they wrote as its prequel, *...cake*, was presented at Theatre Peckham and was nominated for the Alfred Fagon Award in 2021. They co-directed their play *The Master's House* with Chris Sonnex for the National Youth Theatre in 2021, which was shortlisted for the George Devine Award 2022, and developed it into an audio drama for Talawa Stories on BBC Radio 4. In 2022 two of their short plays were presented, *YUMMY*, as part of the Burn It Down festival at Theatre Royal Stratford East and *616: DAWN* as part of Talking about a Revolution at Watford Palace, Lyric Hammersmith Studio and Bristol Old Vic.

babirye is currently under commission to the Yard Theatre and the Royal Court Theatre.

malakaï sargeant | Director

Director malakaï sargeant is a multidisciplinary artist, educator and producer from pre-gentrified northeast London. Led by curiosity and care, malakaï works across theatre, festivals, literature, audio and live events – creating and interrogating through an unapologetically Afroqueer lens. Their work is often non-linear, employing unconventional forms that disrupts notions of time and space; orbiting around ideas of Black interiority, hood surrealism and carceral geographies.

malakaï's directing credits include: *The Master's House* (Talawa/BBC Radio 4/BBC Sounds); *The Costumed Gallery* (UAL/National Gallery); *Still Here?* (Unicorn Theatre); *YUMMY* (Theatre Royal Stratford East); *We Are Here to Make Change* (Royal Court); *...cake* (Theatre Peckham); *Do Nitties Live Forever?* (Battersea Arts Centre); *Over To You* (Tamasha/Rich Mix); *Void* (The S+K Project/Battersea Arts Centre); *I Am Not A ____* (Immediate Theatre/Chat's Palace); *Platform Tottenham* (The S+K Project/Royal Court Theatre/Bernie Grant Arts Centre).

As associate/assistant director their credits include *Hyde and Seek*, directed by Tristan Fynn-Aiduenu (Guildhall School of Music & Drama); *Foxes*, directed by James Hillier (Defibrillator Theatre/

Theatre503); *Calm*, directed by Stella Odunlami (Hackney Empire); *Decolonising History*, directed by Anthony Simpson-Pike (Tamasha/SOAS).

Khadija Raza | Designer

Designer Khadija Raza's selected credits include: *Peanut Butter & Blueberries* (Kiln); *The Secret Garden* (Regents Park Open Air); *Untitled F*ck M*ss S**gon Play* (Royal Exchange/MIF/Headlong/Young Vic); *Girl in the Machine* (Young Vic); *Bach & Sons* (Bridge Theatre); *A History of Water in the Middle East* (Royal Court).

Jahmiko Marshall | Lighting Designer

Jahmiko Marshall is a Lighting and Sound Designer from Bermuda. He obtained his Lighting Technology Certificate from Stagecraft Institute of Las Vegas. He was a student at LAMDA studying towards his BA Hons in Production and Technical Arts.

Mwen | Sound Designer & Composer

Sound Designer and Composer Mwen is a multifaceted artist, working as a theatre sound designer and composer, music producer, and live performing artist. Their creative practice blends the realms of music technology, electronic music, live sound, and performance.

Will Monks | Creative Captions & Video Designer

Creative Captions and Video Designer Will Monks is a London-based lighting and projection designer. His work has accessibility at the heart of it; driven by collaboration and variety, he is always exploring new ways in which the world can be seen.

Asha Jennings-Grant | Intimacy Director & Movement Director

Asha is a Movement Director, Intimacy Coordinator and Intimacy Director for stage and screen. Selected credits include *Moulin Rouge* (Piccadilly Theatre); *MJ: The Musical* (Prince Edward Theatre); *Till the Stars Come Down* (National Theatre); *Romeo and Juliet*, *The Tempest* (Shakespeare's Globe).

Vital Xposure | Producer

For over a decade, Vital Xposure has made disabled-led, radical, political performance championing hidden stories and marginalised voices. From our base in London, we make national-touring, accessible work and position ourselves at the forefront of research and learning around disabled performance. We are committed to a future where marginalised people are recognised, celebrated and empowered as leaders, audiences, participants and artists. Through our work we examine and champion the value of disabled perspectives in our sector. Vital Xposure theatre productions blend cutting-edge performance with powerful storytelling rarely seen on stage. Our pioneering VX Labs research programme explores innovation in access and recontextualises the disabled experience. Informed by a national consultation, VX Labs are delivered in collaboration with regional venues and academic partner Central School of Speech and Drama.

Wellspring, Vital Xposure's talent development initiative showcases the next generation of disabled theatre-makers. From 2022–24, we were proud to support sixteen disabled playwrights in partnership with Hampstead Theatre, Bush Theatre, Soho Theatre, Paines Plough and Theatre503.

Crin Claxon | Production Manager

Crin Claxton is a production manager for theatre choosing to support fringe and political theatre that makes a difference. Crin has worked with companies and venues for over thirty years, including Oval House Theatre, Spare Tyre, Paines Plough, Graeae, Stratford Circus, Vital Xposure, Clean Break, Drunken Chorus, Extant, Oily Cart, Chats Palace, Access All Areas, Lung Theatre, Drake Music, Cardboard Citizens, and Kali Theatre.

Danielle Adéyínká-Uche | Company Stage Manager

Danielle Adéyínká-Uche (she/they) is a powerhouse stage manager and creative force, with skills that stretch across multiple disciplines. A two-time Olivier Award nominee and winner, Danielle brings both vision and technical expertise to the table, ensuring every show hits hard and runs flawlessly.

Joe Colgan | Technical Stage Manager

Joe Colgan, is a UK based Technical/Stage Manager. Previous Film,

Television, and Theatre projects include; Sound No. 2 for film feature and TV, live sound mixing on world premieres. Technical consultant on a variety on touring productions, as well as, Stage Management for national and international touring, musicals and number one selling music artists.

Alison Pottinger | Stage Manager

Alison trained in stage management at Rose Bruford College from 1986-89. From 1999-2002 she retrained as a BSL/English interpreter. Highlights include working with theatres such as Shakespeare's Globe on the first all women of colour production of *Richard II*; Theatre Royal Stratford East; Royal Court; Talawa Theatre; *STARS* by Mojisola Adebayo for Tamasha Theatre; *Reasons to be Cheerful* for Graeae Theatre and *Tommy* for Ramps on the Moon.

Bush Theatre

We make theatre for London. Now.

For over 50 years the Bush Theatre has been a world-famous home for new plays and an internationally renowned champion of playwrights.

Combining ambitious artistic programming with meaningful community engagement work and industry leading talent development schemes, the Bush Theatre champions and supports unheard voices to develop the artists and audiences of the future.

Since opening in 1972 the Bush has produced more than 500 ground-breaking premieres of new plays, developing an enviable reputation for its acclaimed productions nationally and internationally.

They have nurtured the careers of writers including James Graham, Lucy Kirkwood, Temi Wilkey, Jonathan Harvey and Jack Thorne. Recent successes include Tyrell Williams' *Red Pitch*, Benedict Lombe's *Shifters*, and Arinzé Kene's *Misty*. The Bush has won over 100 awards including the Olivier Award for Outstanding Achievement in Affliate Theatre for the past four years for Richard Gadd's *Baby Reindeer*, Igor Memic's *Old Bridge*, Waleed Akhtar's *The P Word* and Matilda Feyiṣayọ Ibini's *Sleepova*.

Located in the renovated old library on Uxbridge Road in the heart of Shepherd's Bush, the Bush Theatre continues to create a space where all communities can be part of its future and call the theatre home.

'The place to go for ground-breaking work as diverse as its audiences' EVENING STANDARD

bushtheatre.co.uk
@bushtheatre

h&f hammersmith & fulham

Arts Council England

Supported by ARTS COUNCIL ENGLAND

rtistic Director	Lynette Linton
ecutive Director	Mimi Findlay
ssociate Artistic Director	Daniel Bailey
eputy Executive Director	Angela Wachner
evelopment & Marketing Assistant	Nicima Abdi
ead of Marketing	Shannon Clarke
ead of Development	Jocelyn Cox
ssociate Dramaturg	Titilola Dawudu
nance Assistant	Lauren Francis
esident Director & Young Company Director	Katie Greenall
echnical & Buildings Manager	Jamie Haigh
eelance Producer	Emma Halstead
ssistant Venue Manager	Rae Harm
ead of Finance	Neil Harris
arketing Officer	Laela Henley-Rowe
ead Producer	Nikita Karia
ommunity Producing Assistant	Joanne Leung
vent Manager	Simon Pilling
enior Technician	John Pullig
oduction Technician	Charlie Sadler
enue Manager (Theatre)	Ade Seriki
ess Manager	Martin Shippen
ommunity Producer	Holly Smith
terary & Producing Assistant	Laetitia Somè
arketing Manager	Ed Theakston
arketing Officer	Kelly Thurston
ssistant Venue Manager (Box Office)	Robin Wilks
heatre Administrator & Executive Assistant	Chloe Wilson
afé Bar Manager	Wayne Wilson

UTY MANAGERS
ara Dawood, Molly Elson, Thomas Ingram, Madeleine Simpson-Kent & nna-May Wood.

ENUE SUPERVISORS
ntony Baker, Addy Caulder-James, Stephanie Cremona, Emma Chatel, ea Hilland, Nzuzi Malemda, Roy Mas, Jacob Meier & Louis Nicholson.

ENUE ASSISTANTS
avine Aduganfi, Doridan Bavangila, Charlotte Binns, Will Byam-Shaw, yerre Clarke, Daniel Fesoom, Matias Hailu, Bo Leandro, Maya Li Preti, hani McGuire, Khy Matinez, April Miller, Ed Mendoza, Carys Murray, Chana ardone, Jennifer Okolo, James Robertson, Ali Shah & Nefertari Williams.

sh Theatre, 7 Uxbridge Road, London W12 8LJ
x Office: 020 8743 5050 | Administration: 020 8743 3584
nail: info@bushtheatre.co.uk | bushtheatre.co.uk

THANK YOU

Our supporters make our work possibl
Together, we're evolving the canon an
creating a bolder, more diverse, an
representative future for British theatr
We're so grateful to you all.

MAJOR DONORS
Charles Holloway OBE
Jim & Michelle Gibson
Georgia Oetker
Cathy & Tim Score
Susie Simkins
Jack Thorne
Gianni & Michael Alen-Buckley

SHOOTING STARS
Jim & Michelle Gibson
Anthony Marraccino & Mariela Manso
Cathy & Tim Score
Susie Simkins

LONE STARS
Clyde Cooper
Adam Kenwright
Jim Marshall
Georgia Oetker

HANDFUL OF STARS
Charlie Bigham
Judy Bollinger
Christopher DelaMare
David des Jardins
Sue Fletcher
Thea Guest
Kate Hamer Ltd
Elizabeth Jack
Simon & Katherine Johnson
Joanna Kennedy
Garry & Lorna Lawrence
Phyllida Lloyd & Kate Pakenham
Vivienne Lukey
Sam & Jim Murgatroyd
Mark & Anne Paterson
Nick & Annie Reid
Bhagat Sharma
Dame Emma Thompson
Joe Tinston & Amelia Knott

RISING STARS
Elizabeth Beebe
Matthew Cushen
Anne-Hélène and Rafaël Biosse Duplan
Martin Blackburn
David Brooks
Catharine Browne
Anthony Chantry
Lauren Clancy
Richard & Sarah Clarke
Caroline Clasen
Susan Cuff
Austin Erwin
Kim Evans
Mimi Findlay
Jack Gordon
Hugh & Sarah Grootenhuis
Sarah Harrison
Uzma Hasan
Lesley Hill & Russ Shaw
Davina & Malcolm Judelson
Mike Lewis
Lynette Linton
Michael McCoy
Judy Mellor
Caro Millington
Rajiv Nathwani
Yoana Nenova
Stephen Pidcock
Miguel & Valeri Ramos Handal
James St. Ville KC
Jan Topham
Kit & Anthony van Tulleken
Evanna White
Ben Yeoh

CORPORATE SPONSORS
Biznography
Casting Pictures Ltd.
Nick Hern Books
S&P Global
The Agency

TRUSTS & FOUNDATIONS
Backstage Trust
Buffini Chao Foundation
Christina Smith Foundatior
Daisy Trust
Esmée Fairbairn Foundatio
The Foyle Foundation
Garfield Weston Foundatio
Garrick Charitable Trust
Hammersmith United Charities
The Harold Hyam Wingate Foundation
Idlewild Trust
Jerwood Foundation
John Lyon's Charity
Martin Bowley Charitable Trust
Noël Coward Foundation
Royal Victoria Hall Foundation
The Thistle Trust

And all the donors who wish to remain anonymous.

If you are interested in finding out how to be involved, please visit **bushtheatre.co.uk/support-u** email **development@bushtheatre.co.uk** or call **020 8743 3584**.

…blackbird hour

babirye bukilwa

For Eshes and their boats x

This is dedicated to all the versions of me who have died:
thank you for coming, holding and keeping me here.
To all the versions of me I will meet:
thank you for your patience, forgiveness, grace and tenacity.

Thanks

I would like to thank the following people for shaping this fruit: adoudu', Adrian Gardner, Akiya Henry, Amarachi Nwokoro, Ashden Oke, Azuka Okafor, Cherrelle Skeete, Daniel Ward, Deji Tiwo, Donna Banya, EJ Saunders, Emeka Sesay, Emmanuel Ogunijinmi, Eshe Asante, Femi Tiwo, Gail Babb, Iman Xashi, Jane Fallowfield, Joy Gharoro-Akpojotor, Kamara Scott, Kariima Ali, Khaleb Luan Brooks, Kimberley Okoye, Lorna Fallowfield, Louise Mayse, Martins Imhangbe, Michael Balogun, Michael Buffong, Mimi Findlay, Miranda Cromwell, Mohammed Manasray, Myah Jeffers, Naeem Davis, Nambi Kiyira, Nkechinyere Nwobani-Akanwo, Pepter Lunkuse, Rianna Jade Parker, Rob Ellis, Ruka Johnson, Ryan Mayse, Seye Isikalu, Shalisha Jennifer, Stella Magento, Susan Wokoma, Talawa Theatre Company, Tania Nwachukwu, Nottingham Playhouse Cherry Orchard Acting Company 2017, Tunji Lucas, Unique Spencer, X-BAG, Yami 'Rowdy' Lofvenberg, Yrsa Daley Ward, my twin sister Yvonne and my big sister Vivian.

I would like to highlight the following people for their generosity, patience, care and belief in my many forms, selves and contradictions: Vital Exposure, the Bush Theatre, Stephen Bailey, Imogen Sarre, Olivia Nakintu, Evelyn Oyedokun, Danielle Kassaraté and Ivan Oyik.

And to malakaï sargeant: you found me in Atlantis, thank you for reminding me that I can glow in the dark.

young seeds that have not seen sun
forget
and drown easily.

Audre Lorde, 'Coping'

'You will never break generational
curses if the generation is still cursed
and their approval is required.'

future me

Characters

ESHE, *Black, dark-skinned, twenty-seven, invisible disability*
ELLA, *Black, dark-skinned, thirty-two*
MICHAEL, *Black, dark-skinned, twenty-seven*
SISSY VOICE, *Black, dark-skinned, an ancestor*

Note on the Text

… indicates painful thoughts

– indicates thoughts unspoken

/ indicates an interruption of thought or dialogue

[xxxxxx] indicates words not said but for context

Note

this is not a play about inverted comma mental health inverted comma nor is it an Angry Black Women issue play

This text went to press before the end of rehearsals and so may differ slightly from the play as performed.

ACT ONE

… the boat

3.33 a.m.

December 8th 2016.

Bethnal Green.

floating

Thunder and crashing rain.

In fact it's a (brain)storm.

ESHE *is alone.*

She wears an oversized T-shirt.

She wears one sock and underwear.

No bra. The space is filled with water.

Glitter.

She's got some kind of sailor hat on, maybe a pirate hat or one of those colonial sailing hats used in navy propaganda.

It rests on top of a wig.

She has a bag with her full of 'important things'.

She has a flask of brandy in her hand

and something boaty, maybe a sailing paddle in the other hand.

ESHE *has a bandage on her left knee*

and a phone/torch

a portable radio

(fishing rod?)

(a waterproof jacket?)

a small alarm clock.

floating in the water

rocking back and forth with the (brain)waves.

ESHE *attempts to find signal.*

She can't.

ESHE *attempts to find signal.*

She can't.
She can't.

SISSY VOICE. can't reach you.

ESHE *throws her phone in the ocean.*

won't reach me.

ESHE. you never wanted to be reached.

SISSY VOICE. can't reach me

ESHE. you never wanna be got

SISSY VOICE. can't cop me

ESHE. [you] cut your antenna.

thawed your branches

SISSY VOICE. i reach dem

ESHE. who's dem?

SISSY VOICE. i reach me

ESHE. which dem

SISSY VOICE. roses don't have branches

ESHE. which you?

SISSY VOICE. roses don't have antenna

ESHE. they do. and roots. roses have roots.

SISSY VOICE. who's buying you roses, that silly little michael?

ESHE. silly little me

SISSY VOICE. my ex-girlfriend's son eshe?

ESHE. he's not hers or mine

SISSY VOICE. you always talking in rhyme

ESHE. you started in poesy.

SISSY VOICE. you're not smart

ESHE. i'm unbelievable mum. unbelievable.

ESHE *goes into her bag and pulls out a brandy bottle and sips.*
She also sets her alarm clock to an hour and places it on the side of the boat so she can hear it.
ESHE *turns her pocket radio on in an attempt to find the perfect song.*
Nina Simone's 'Don't Smoke in Bed' plays.

SISSY VOICE. dramatic

ESHE. yeah

ESHE *sips.*

SISSY VOICE. big tune

ESHE. so big it doesn't have a form

ESHE *sings along for a moment. It's quite beautiful.*

She plays faux piano.

She makes shadow puppets.

She can sing. Really really well.

It does become too much.

She smells her armpits.

She pinches herself.

She slaps herself.

She pulls out some balloons and she blows them up.

She plays with them.

She pulls out a small cupcake.

She lights a candle and blows it out.

glitter

nausea

dance

sway

shapes

stillness

dance

dance

Joy

her paddle becoming a microphone.

Her alarm clock the truth.

Her balloons; her witnesses.

Tiptoes.

Her boat a courtroom.

ESHE *sings this to us*

to dem

stim

to it

to all

her boat her own.

She lights a pre-rolled spliff.

glitter

Drinks.

Gulps
gulps

stim

She enjoys that fucking spliff.

The song ends.

sorry

Toto's 'Africa' plays. Maybe the chorus – it is the worst part of the song. Maybe just the 'dum dum dum de dum dum dum'.

absolutely fucking not.

ESHE*'s phone rings. She ignores it.*

Bobby Brown's 'My Prerogative' plays.

yeah okay.

ESHE *reaches inside the walls of the boat and starts to throw things out of it.*

A half-eaten apple

crisp packets

magazines

socks

toothbrushes

pillows

fried-chicken boxes

tissue

Rizla

nicotine

cigarette butts

lamb patty

empty pho container

pizza boxes

ESHE*'s phone rings.*

cutlery *dishes*

dishes

dishes

cups

mirror

mugs

tarot cards

crystals

paints

Phone ringing.

vibrating

crystals

sage

painkillers

shoes

a notepad and pen. *She rejoices.*

Another swig of brandy.

maybe another

ESHE *begins writing a letter.*
It's difficult.

SISSY VOICE. that about me?

ESHE *changes the station and it's white noise? Maybe radio murmurs? Maybe something sad.*

ESHE *finds writing this letter extremely difficult.*
She lights sage
it rains

(*maybe flowers*)

ESHE *slaps herself.*

ESHE *stims.*

She makes it to the end of the letter.

ESHE*'s phone rings again.*

And her boat stops floating.

A knocking can be heard.

ESHE*'s boat has disappeared. An interruption.*

It's stopped raining.

She has stopped floating.

For a moment ESHE *is just* ESHE.

(Brain)storm interrupted with:

ELLA. i got you roses!

ELLA *appears. Soaking wet with a rucksack on, bike helmet and a dinghy.*

SISSY VOICE. she still around?

ESHE. …

ELLA. esh? eshe? i have my key darling. but i want to. i want to respect your boundaries. and privacy… erm.

eshe? eshe my darling? love? can you let me in? am i allowed inside please?

ESHE. –

ELLA. esh? just… it's been pouring outside. and…

i am respecting your boundaries! honouring your boundaries with an 's'. i am. i. i umm. i did call. and i've text you sweetheart. i've been calling but you… i've been trying to contact you sweetheart to communicate. i can see that you're – i. i know you're up. it's your time.

ESHE. –

ELLA. …

ESHE. –

SISSY VOICE. what time is it eshe?

ELLA. witching hour! i was researching, i do listen and i did listen. and i've been researching actually. a lot actually. about.

about time, and and and process and about witching hours in indigenous cultures! and yes. umm how for certain societies and subcultures. well people really and – not that you're a person – you are whatever you want to be!

ESHE.… / …

ELLA. and the time of three a.m. is quite. it's umm, it's a time of liminality for lots of… shit.

ELLA *listens.*

ESHE *smokes.*

i can see your light on

ESHE *switches off her torch.*

my ears still work

ESHE *pauses the static.*

i just wanna know you're okay.

you sounded really upset and in a way that really really concerned me… i care about you

…

i just wanna know you're okay please?

that you're alright… you know? not…

and then i'll go.

ESHE *smokes.*

i can't leave until you show me you're okay so please come to the door. i won't leave babe! not leaving! look, i'm here. i'm here on our street. under the moon. under the…

like just stick your head in the door frame or show me a thumbs-up. a toe. something.

ESHE. –

ELLA. i'm sorry.

ESHE....

ELLA. fuck

ESHE. –

ELLA. –

ESHE. –

ELLA. i didn't mean what i said. and i didn't mean to end things. well i. i didn't mean for it to come out like that, in that particular way in that particular – i felt cornered okay? and lied to massively… and you didn't say. you didn't tell me… and i had to go and find it out.

i felt gaslit! oww

ELLA *has a small coughing fit.*

fucking. ow. oh goodness. i think i have a chest infection. well i know, i know i have a chest infection because i'm on antibiotics at the moment so i'm /

ELLA *coughs.*

dead. feel dead. god. but it's not the same. i know this. i'm not saying we are the same at all. or. or that that me and you go through the same thing. but sometimes it feels like.

like it's a.

ELLA *coughs.*

fuck! my lungs esh. my chest. and. so.

yes so i was thinking about viruses and bacteria of the human body essentially and like how. i dunno.

… (*A noise of exasperation.*)

phlegm?

how phlegm can be treated in various ways but you need to know that it's there. like being infected. the infection. in order for you to treat it, the 'it' here being the infection, in order for me to take the antibiotics i have to accept that it's there. the infection. and then past accepting. let me gather my thoughts. okay. transposition really.

it's then about transmuting from acceptance to action. action here meaning like, getting rid of it. anyways. fuck. like fuck basically have i just been walking around as a giant phlegm.

or is the phlegm in me.

you're not phlegm to me.

you're not.

…

ESHE *opens the door for a soaking* ELLA.
ELLA *offers her dinghy to* ESHE.
ESHE *does not accept.*
The dinghy transforms into black roses.
ESHE*'s bedroom walls appear.*
ESHE*'s paddle now becomes a crutch.*

…

ESHE. –

ELLA.…

ESHE. –

ELLA.…

ESHE.…

ELLA. we can stay in the dark if you want.

SISSY VOICE. patronising

ELLA *hovers.*
ELLA *takes in the room.*
It smells.
It is a mess.
ELLA*'s skin crawls.*
ELLA *wants to open a window.*
ESHE *watches* ELLA.
ESHE *demonstrates her anger passive-aggressively.*
ESHE *takes some painkillers.*

ELLA. do you need some water to take those?

ESHE *takes them with some brandy.*

can help you clean up a bit? i can do the dishes

SISSY VOICE *makes a sound like a panting dog.*

ESHE *smokes.*

ESHE. –

ELLA. fresh bed sheets?

ESHE. –

ELLA. don't have to talk it's okay. you can just. point. point me in the. rubbish? it's fine. we can stay like this. it's fine. put your clothes away? open a window?

ESHE. whayou come ere for?

SISSY VOICE. everyone loves the show. hates the actor

ESHE. love the playwright hate the play?

ELLA. i wanted to make sure you were okay

ESHE. verdict

SISSY VOICE *does the sound of wrong answer.*

ELLA. you haven't answered my calls

ESHE. –

ELLA. or my texts

ESHE. –

ELLA. or anything really love

ESHE. –

ELLA. it's important. and i know it's hard when you're having a. going through a /

ESHE. what? you know it's hard when i'm having a what. going through a what?

ELLA.…

ESHE.…

ELLA. have you reached your basic needs today?

ESHE *sips.*

sun. water. you stretched?

ESHE. –

ELLA. i'm trying eshe… i'm still processing. i have my processes too

ESHE *sips.*

ESHE. –

ELLA. [i'll] just open the windows

ESHE. –

ELLA. take the bins out and. what do you need?

ESHE. –

ELLA. if you don't tell me how can i help?

ESHE. –

ELLA. –

ESHE.…

ELLA. please. anything. just ask.

ESHE *stands.*
ESHE *opens her arms, asking for a hug.*

ELLA *watches.*
ESHE *makes her arms wider.*

ELLA *does not hug* ESHE.

ESHE.…

ESHE *plays something passive-aggressive, maybe it's gospel music or something pop-y.*

SISSY VOICE. can't reach dem

ESHE *plays with some balloons.*
Maybe she throws them at ELLA.
Maybe she throws them at us.

ELLA *doesn't know what to do.*

She takes off her rucksack and pulls out a box that has 'Good Days' with one of the Os faded out.

She goes to give it to ESHE.

She can't.

ELLA. i found this at yours. thought it would be helpful. you can stay here for as long you need, my parents don't mind me at theirs. i mean that.

ELLA *places the roses on top of the box.*

ESHE*'s windows and ceiling appear.*

–

ESHE. –

ELLA. –

ESHE. –

She leaves it next to the door.
It's not easy.
ELLA *leaves.*

ESHE *laughs.*

ESHE *screams.*

ESHE *puts the lights on.*

Her room is a mess.

It's painful to see.

ESHE *sees dem.*

ESHE *sees us.*

ESHE *sees it.*
And dem. And it.

ESHE *hears dem.*

you man gonna do anything. just there yamming my brain. yamming loudly. like it's your favourite dish, your favourite delight.

SISSY VOICE. nobody's reaching you

ESHE. i know.

SISSY VOICE. nobody reaches us

ESHE. alright mum. alright

ESHE *drinks some more brandy.*

ESHE *changes the song. Again.*

ESHE *changes her hairstyle.*

ESHE *changes her T-shirt.*

ESHE *draws on her own arms.*

ESHE *creams her face.*

ESHE *doodles.*

ESHE*'s phone rings.*

ESHE *declines.*

ESHE *gets a text.*

ESHE *starts to sing.*

ESHE *gets a text.*

ESHE *cries.*

okay but what are you actually leaving? nothing and no one sustainable.

ESHE *reads her phone, searching for what she is leaving. It's the opposite of empowering.*

'congratulations on your one-thousandth retweet.' okay
(*lists*) black excellence
black excellence
black excellence
black men being disappointing
black women being embarrassing
black excellence
black excellence
sanism
rah bare people have watched this.
bare people are watching this

and war
nothing.

ESHE *becomes overwhelmed with dizziness.*
Her head feels heavy.
She tries to deep-breathe.
ESHE *looks to her 'God Day' box.*
Collecting one of her crutches, she uses it to bring the box next to her.
She smells it.
She is whole somehow.
She opens this box with the delicacy of stroking a kitten.
She rummages.
Astrology books.
A photo album.
A DVD.
Cassette tapes.
Old rings.
Contents of an altar.
I Know Why the Caged Bird Sings *by Maya Angelou.*
The Master's Tools Will Never Dismantle the Master's House *by Audre Lorde.*
Some letters.
And lastly a vinyl.

She takes the vinyl out of the slip and holds it in front of her.
With one deep intake of breath she snaps the record into pieces.
She stares at these pieces.

SISSY VOICE. why you do that for?

ESHE. fucking shut up fuck fuck

ESHE *sips.*

She plays Eternal's 'Stay'. She attempts the long 'staaaaaaaaaay'.

She ad-libs the song, sometimes changing the lyrics.

stay baby
stay, come on darling now
stay, you know i want you back

stay with me tonight
come on won't you stay
stay, oh
stay
stay with me

it seems i got a fucked-up mind
can someone help me finnnnnnd?
baby girl has left meeee
i'm always getting left behinnnnnnd
I don't know, I don't know nobody knows /

ESHE*'s phone starts vibrating.*
She declines the call.

(*Shouting/singing.*) how long?! how long.

Her phone rings a different ringtone.

mike!

SISSY VOICE. eeeeeeeeeedyat boy

ESHE. michael

SISSY VOICE *kisses her teeth.*

ESHE *picks up.*
ESHE *pauses the music.*
ESHE *slurs.*
ESHE*'s kitchen and doors appear.*

man like, man like mike…
when i grow up i wanna be just like
ah zim zimma who go the keys to my bimma
i said: who got the keys to my bimma?!
…
you're supposed to sing it back been thinking about you too bro
you been speaking to ella?…
why?
…
what did she say?
laughable
wow…

she won't leave me alone.
obsessive. possessive.
she's a fucking…
what?…
i'm fine michael. no problem
no problem
…
huh?
i didn't ask her to come here.
no…
when was the last time you guys even spoke?…
i don't have a problem with it. no problem
it's fine…
nobody asked her to show up in the middle of the night with her feelings about chest
her chest or something. she's a fucking –
no. i'm fine mike… yeah, mans is still here b… a societal pillar. statue. ornament
…
feel like a painting. gawped at.
never engaged with
like.
just high value no autonomy. okay.
why did you call me
no don't. i want to be alone. with my own brain and that.
why did you call me.
you called me because of ella?
you keep asking me the same question and wanting a different answer. like people call *me* mad bro. are *you* okay bredrin?
yes i have a charger iphone…
of course you are…
don't knock, don't knock. only feds and suits knock on doors bro

ESHE *opens the door for* MICHAEL.
She stands defiantly in her all.
He takes her in. His car keys in his hand.
She takes him in.

MICHAEL. –

ESHE. –

MICHAEL.…

ESHE.…

MICHAEL.…

MICHAEL *opens his arms as to offer a hug.*

SISSY VOICE. moist yute michael

ESHE *does not accept the hug.*
MICHAEL *eyes* ESHE.
ESHE *demonstrates anger and sadness.*
Maybe she turns her back to him.
Maybe she screams silently.
Maybe she pretends to cry and then laughs about it.
Maybe she pretends to choke herself or shoot herself in the head.
Maybe she cries and collects her tears and wipes them on his chest.
Maybe she just stares through him.

MICHAEL *comes into the room.*
He takes it in.
He takes ESHE *in.*
He pulls out a lighter and an incense stick.
He lights it.
He knows where to put it.
ESHE *offers him a spliff.*
MICHAEL *declines.*
She walks over to him and offers the spliff again.
He takes it.
He needed that. Like really fucking 'ohhh my sweet fanny' needed that.
He smokes.
ESHE *gets him an empty glass and places a brandy bottle next to him.*
He doesn't touch it.
MICHAEL *watches* ESHE.

ESHE. what flavour is that?

MICHAEL *smokes.*

smells nice

MICHAEL *smokes.*

how was that?

MICHAEL. –

ESHE. i know you hate speaking to her so.

MICHAEL.…

ESHE. –

MICHAEL.…

ESHE. put stillness on that to-do list?

MICHAEL. –

ESHE. survey on that to do list?

drink?

MICHAEL.…

ESHE. it's henny.

MICHAEL.…

ESHE. nice to see you

MICHAEL. yeah?

ESHE. nice to see you; seeing me. yeah

MICHAEL. –

ESHE *takes him in.*

SISSY VOICE. he wants to fuck.

ESHE. hmm

SISSY VOICE. all they ever want is to f/uck

ESHE. been going gym or something?

SISSY VOICE. watch you and fu/ck you

ESHE. you look like you been going gym

MICHAEL. –

ESHE. silence

MICHAEL.…

ESHE. –

MICHAEL.…

ESHE. wanna charge your phone den?

MICHAEL. –

ESHE. –

MICHAEL. –

ESHE. why you here mike?

MICHAEL. –

ESHE.…

MICHAEL. she's concerned about you

SISSY VOICE. he speaks

ESHE. – …

MICHAEL. really concerned

ESHE. she concerns herself with concern

MICHAEL. what happened eshe?

ESHE. life innit

MICHAEL. what's that mean?

ESHE. you tell me mike

MICHAEL. –

ESHE. you tell me, what you think i mean when i say that.

MICHAEL. i dunno

ESHE. –

MICHAEL. but i wanna know eshe

ESHE. –

MICHAEL. that's why i'm asking.

ESHE. –

ESHE *drinks.*

MICHAEL. –

ESHE. well you've checked on me now

MICHAEL. –

ESHE. thanks

MICHAEL. you're welcome

ESHE. you've seen i'm breathing. you can go and report back

MICHAEL. what you doing?

ESHE. tell them. whoever. tell the street and the pope that i've reached my basic needs or whatever however

MICHAEL. what are you doing

ESHE. watching you watch me mike

MICHAEL. this what we gonna do?

ESHE. what we doin?

MICHAEL.…

ESHE. what are we doing

MICHAEL. –

ESHE. i asked you a question

MICHAEL. i answer yours you don't answer mine? i don't enjoy talking to her…

ESHE. –

MICHAEL. it's not fun

ESHE.…

MICHAEL. i don't like it

ESHE. you didn't have to pick up the call mike.

MICHAEL. –

ESHE. obsessive… what's the point of you right now?

MICHAEL. the point?

ESHE. yes. the point. the function. utility. purpose. role / province. duty

MICHAEL. we know you're smart eshe

ESHE *finds this amusing.*

we all know how smart you are

ESHE. and you all hate it

MICHAEL. i don't

ESHE. i'm not tryna be smart

MICHAEL. you are. since your new ting yeah. your new sit[uation], you been caring about and do care about sounding smart acting / smart

ESHE. i'm just reading books michael.

MICHAEL. from where.

ESHE. i'm full of books michael, scriptures.

MICHAEL. i've read your poetry. still read it

ESHE. school took the majority of our childhood and made us prison guards of our own prison

MICHAEL. [what the actual fuck?]

ESHE. we treat our bodies like how the coloniser treats the land

MICHAEL. okay

ESHE. you don't get it

SISSY VOICE. he'll never get you

MICHAEL. i do. but i don't care about the words you know and the words you can pick together. put together like. i don't care about dem tings. regular talk and regular you. regular degular you. ordinary you. so i did have to pick up the phone to her cos it's you

ESHE. i'm not regular.

MICHAEL. yeah obviously that's what i'm saying / you're special to me

ESHE. don't get treated regular.

MICHAEL. precious and special to me

ESHE. don't get looked at regular.

MICHAEL. okay

ESHE. don't even get treated like a woman. not seen as woman-shaped. not woman recognised.

SISSY VOICE. why you crying

ESHE. don't you get it?

MICHAEL. get what?

ESHE. i understand

MICHAEL. understand what

SISSY VOICE. what do *you* know. what do you know

ESHE. i understand i am not regular. michael i don't want to be regular. i can't be. i've tried.

ESHE *drinks.*

MICHAEL. i'm not her

ESHE. who?

MICHAEL. and i hate what she's turned you into

ESHE. turned?

MICHAEL. eshe look at me. you're not okay

ESHE. *she* hasn't… mans is here. mans been here

MICHAEL. you said she came in and saw you

ESHE. who

MICHAEL. ella

ESHE. yep

MICHAEL. and she left?

ESHE. mhm

MICHAEL. –

ESHE. –

MICHAEL. she left you

ESHE. [yes]

MICHAEL. doesn't look like she's been here

ESHE. what's that mean

MICHAEL *gestures the room.*

SISSY VOICE. clean house clean thoughts

MICHAEL.…

ESHE. whayou here for?

SISSY VOICE. clean thoughts clean house

MICHAEL. she said that you've started drinking again?

ESHE. i stopped?

MICHAEL. heavily

ESHE. *heavily*

MICHAEL. copious

ESHE. what man know about the word copious

MICHAEL. eshe

ESHE. you like saying my name innit?

MICHAEL. i like you being alive.

ESHE *demonstrates that she is alive. Maybe she tap-dances.*
Maybe she does a silly dance.
Maybe she tries to joke about.
Maybe she bites her arm.
MICHAEL *is amused.*

you're not regular i get it

ESHE. reggy deggy; small ordinary. sloppy nothing scripted hero saviour script black man scripted.

MICHAEL. mad ting

ESHE. indeed. what did you and your good friend ella have to chat about at this hour?

MICHAEL. –

ESHE. tell me

MICHAEL. we didn't even talk for long

ESHE. got a lot to say

MICHAEL. she called me. don't even have her number saved. we don't talk. you know that.

SISSY VOICE. do you?

ESHE. shut up! do i? it's news to me that you and my ex-fucking-girlfriend seem to be having 'eshe's gone crazy chats' late at night b. news to fucking / me

MICHAEL. nobody is calling you crazy.

SISSY VOICE. well that's a lie

MICHAEL. you hate her

SISSY VOICE. that's a lie too

ESHE.…

MICHAEL. i hate her

ESHE. liar

MICHAEL. i fucking hate her.

ESHE *drinks quite a lot.*

right now?

ESHE. *you* came here

MICHAEL. –

ESHE. so what i am doing. is me. let me have my things. in my own space

MICHAEL. that's not a thing

ESHE. i'm an adult michael

MICHAEL. that and you don't mix well

ESHE. thanks mister doctor

MICHAEL. that and you mix like oil and water

ESHE. maybe i want to be not-quite-mixed oily water? my own thing a new thing. maybe i wanna be a thing. a formless nameless thing.

MICHAEL. self-obliteration

ESHE. so *you* can read new books

MICHAEL. self-mutilation.

ESHE. but i have to reread the same ones? old gospels?

MICHAEL. break-ups are rough. let it be fresh. let the wound be fresh

ESHE *sings the first line of the chorus of OutKast's 'So Fresh, So Clean'.*

MICHAEL *joins in with the backing vocals.*

ESHE. there you are

ESHE *offers* MICHAEL *a drink.*

MICHAEL. i know you're going through a lot at the moment

ESHE. there you went

MICHAEL. you're still... getting yourself back together innit and i feel guilt/y

ESHE. you taking observational classes?

MICHAEL. eshe i'm tryna say /

ESHE. to be fair you always were observant

MICHAEL. can you listen to me?

ESHE. i am. you knew i loved her before i did

MICHAEL. do you wanna listen to me?

ESHE. no. you knew i would fall and fumble all over / her

MICHAEL. tryna say sorry like, i didn't come to talk bout her

ESHE. and yet…

MICHAEL. i came here for you

ESHE. i'm actually very much okay. so. or i'm not. and that seems to be hard for people to deal with and i think i don't give a fuck and i'm actually. actually tired of giving a fuck about it. and empathising with people who find me… so. so. [thank] you for coming. i'll roll you a spliff for your travels

ESHE *goes to roll a spliff.*

MICHAEL. eshe

ESHE. –

MICHAEL. i'm here b

ESHE. i'm really good at spliffs

MICHAEL. i'm here.

ESHE. –

MICHAEL. do you always need that [spliff]?

ESHE. cry me an ocean

MICHAEL. you don't always have to take yourself somewhere

ESHE. i'm in atlantis b

MICHAEL. –

ESHE. but you man ain't hearing

MICHAEL. wherever you are. i love you

SISSY VOICE *makes a vomit noise.*

ESHE. boring

MICHAEL. i love you

ESHE. bore and a chore

MICHAEL. i do

ESHE. why do people keep saying that?

MICHAEL. i do love you

ESHE. why do people keep meaning it

MICHAEL. who is people

ESHE. means nothing. meaning it. *meaning* your love to me, means nothing to me here.

MICHAEL. okay

ESHE. i'm unmoved unevolved.

MICHAEL. you drank water?

ESHE. about 'i love you'

MICHAEL *makes* ESHE *a drink of water.*

about 'you don't have to do drugs to deal with pain'. got any other ideas sherlock?

MICHAEL. here

ESHE. got any other bullet points for me to bullet point on my mind map of 'how to stay fucking alive'

MICHAEL. drink it

ESHE. 'get well soon' songs and 'love yourself through the pain' poems? i can put them on post-its! great idea

SISSY VOICE. drink it

ESHE. oh shut up!

MICHAEL. i get it

ESHE. pink and yellow post-it notes!

MICHAEL. eshe

ESHE. never thought of that

MICHAEL. listen to me please

ESHE. lists will cure me. oh wise wise michael. thank you

MICHAEL. alright.

ESHE. why you shouting?

MICHAEL. –

ESHE. the door

MICHAEL. what has she done to you?

ESHE. who is she

MICHAEL. and what did she say to you

ESHE. what she?

MICHAEL. what did ella do here.

ESHE. [nothing]

MICHAEL. it's been a rough year since your mum [died]

ESHE. why do you have to put this on any of dem

MICHAEL. i'm only saying that if you take a step / back

ESHE. don't put this [what is happening here] on ella. or my mum. or you. or this [alcohol]. or or. i'm. i'm this is mine. for me. you don't and she doesn't and they don't get to.

MICHAEL. what?

ESHE. my brain is my brain. okay. this is… i get to have this, can't trade it. for me. it's mine and me. and dem. many selves.

SISSY VOICE. you're theirs.

ESHE. i'm mine. and it's me. am i making sense?

MICHAEL. you are beautiful. and lovable

ESHE. yes. love able. i'm very much something to love

MICHAEL. yes.

SISSY VOICE. no one is listening.

ESHE. i'm very much someone to be listened to

MICHAEL. i'm listening

ESHE. i'm.

SISSY VOICE. gone on. use your words. use your words eshe. big mouth. big chest big words.

MICHAEL. you're?

ESHE. red

SISSY VOICE. no

ESHE. faces. water

SISSY VOICE. and? and? and?

ESHE*'s bedroom is flooding.*
Only ESHE *can see this.*

MICHAEL. and?

ESHE.…

MICHAEL *opens his arms to hug* ESHE.

please leave

MICHAEL. no

ESHE. please leave

MICHAEL. no

ESHE. fuck. i've got eyes michael they do still work

MICHAEL. likkle one two hoover and bang.

ESHE. can you hoover this? look at me. look in me. please. with your anything-but-regular eyes. anything-but-regular context about who i am and what i am. please be real with me. take a good look… nasty innit? say it.

MICHAEL. no

ESHE. you're a liar

MICHAEL. you're not nasty to me

ESHE. you are simple and a liar

MICHAEL. seen

ESHE. least i could feel the repugnance in ella. ick. longing loathing of / lingering

MICHAEL. you have so many amazing qualities!

ESHE. name them!

MICHAEL. i'll be here forever

ESHE. with chest! name them.

MICHAEL. you make everyone around you better /

ESHE. ha! /

MICHAEL. you've made me a better man you've made ella a better woman

ESHE. it's not my fucking job or birthright to be the mother africa mammy teacher priest healer with never-ending breast milk and wet narn to make you a better man. fuck you.

MICHAEL. i didn't mean it / like that

ESHE. you did mean it like that

MICHAEL. you want me to hate you. you want me to call you everything you call yourself

ESHE. you are the same sentence over and over again.

ESHE *takes a pill.*
MICHAEL *drinks.*

– you ever see someone unlove you in slow motion? unlove you in real time to your face in your face?

MICHAEL. …nah

ESHE. every time she looks at me i feel the shame of her mum and her mum's mum… i physically feel her essence recoil. i never have to second-guess 'tolerance' my g. crystal clear. but you /

MICHAEL. i'm sorry she makes you feel that way. i don't feel that way about you

ESHE. you look at me like i give you oxygen. i am anaerobic bacteria

ESHE *drinks.*

MICHAEL. i'm not leaving

ESHE. can't you feel it? smell it?

MICHAEL *opens a window.*

i stink mike, i smell so bad… i haven't showered in… days? weeks maybe. i can't remember. ain't brushed my teeth…

MICHAEL. –

ESHE. i tried to. my bottom teeth. hurt. they started bleeding… and the colour. red. painful. it's painful to brush them.

MICHAEL.…

ESHE. i'm gross michael

MICHAEL. i'm sorry you're feeling this way

ESHE. you sound like you work at a morgue.

MICHAEL. what

ESHE. or marks and spencers

MICHAEL. what

ESHE. you aren't doing anything useful. what have you done since you been here? ain't washed nothing. moved nothing around.

MICHAEL. i'm being here for you /

ESHE. just standing. just smoking up, blazing up / using up my weed

MICHAEL. here with you as you are / in this

ESHE. and breathing in my air. tall in your nothing. confident in your nothing. impressing on my ting, surveying my own real tings, that are mine. big arms. and big self. for what. why are you here.

MICHAEL. i wanna help. i hate seeing you like this man. i'm in love with you eshe.

ESHE. this love word

MICHAEL. el-oh-vee-ee

ESHE. do people use it when they feel sorry? scared.

MICHAEL. no.

ESHE. is that what were doing now. swapping love for safety

MICHAEL. no

ESHE. you can't stand that however you feel about me doesn't change that i wanna combust into brilliant black dust. so you ignore my desires and throw in a four-letter word that you don't even know how to use? where to use it and for what? i don't need to be pacified michael. i'm not a child.

MICHAEL. you use language like a weapon sometimes

ESHE. it is.

MICHAEL. you use language like you're fighting

ESHE. i am. you know it's a question. you use 'i love you'. like it's a question.

MICHAEL. i don't mind asking it

ESHE. i think the first person who ever told me that they loved me lied.

MICHAEL. they never taught us how to love us. sissy tried her best

SISSY VOICE. always liked that brudda

ESHE. you ever get punished for being smart?

MICHAEL. what's that mean?

ESHE. what about smart and beautiful

MICHAEL. people think i'm dumb. like you. you think i'm dumb

ESHE. i'm tired of talking about her / thinking about her

MICHAEL. who's her?

ESHE. ruminating her. smelling her. hearing her. hearing dem. it's tiring.

MICHAEL. do you hear me? do *you* hear *me* eshe?

MICHAEL *offers* ESHE *a hug.*

SISSY VOICE. das conditional eshe

ESHE *takes* MICHAEL*'s hand, places it on her chest and then throws his hand away.*

ESHE *drinks.*

–

ESHE. everyone's profoundly deep, every fucking one

MICHAEL. –

ESHE. and then they're not

MICHAEL. –

ESHE. language is all we

MICHAEL. –

ESHE. words

MICHAEL. i'm here. they never taught us how to love us.

ESHE. i don't want love

MICHAEL. they didn't. /

ESHE. i don't want you here

MICHAEL. i've been reading some of the books you leant me

ESHE. jellyfish.

MICHAEL. they are in my car.

ESHE. i want to be a jellyfish

ICHAEL. and listen our parents, like our mums they did their best / but they

ESHE *bangs her head against a wall. Quite a few times.*

ESHE. i don't want your limericks and lyrics and theory; this love, that 'love', don't reach here, yeah? doesn't lurk here.

so i go out and look, search; love-hunting. but it doesn't translate to me. different language. like my tongue don't. can't. read it. i might reach it, maybe. touch it. ow. ow. but it hurts all over. a trap. trapping. pulling apart my skin. it. it smothers me. this love; your love, that you want me, to want, and you want me to fight for – nigga it *strangles* you. love has you waking up in the middle of the night in a panic. has you feeling half. niggas out here walking around like half a person, brudda.

so i amputate myself. rejig. reshape. i squish my tail into my stomach through my throat. stand tall: brace. put on radioactive love armour cos. fuck. it's like. i gotta separate myself and my selves. and the people and places that make me me. and it's still not. and i run. sprint. and still. and it's still. stealing…

love feels like catholic shame. a never-healing wound. it invades your white blood cells. your gums and skin. hair follicles. the corners of your belly that you didn't even know existed. love makes you want. forever. love erupts your identity, makes promises, lies, feasts. love suffocates. i've read it front to back and in latin. you man are reading chapters and not getting to the end. what about you? you got to the end?

MICHAEL. bell hooks says /

ESHE. take my knickers

MICHAEL. what

ESHE. take my knickers michael

MICHAEL. –

ESHE. –

MICHAEL. –

ESHE. you el-oh-vee-ee me. right? all of me yeah? the good and the beautiful bits? the endearing bits. the regular bits. the bits you used to find lovely and sweet and revolutionary and radical and beautiful and worthy. loved so much, in awe so much you would have put me in a vase. on display. and then you realise i need water and sunlight and i have roots and i'm not a *thing* that was *made* with quirky interchangeable glow-in-the-dark fridge magnets. you find out i'm real. full. then then, then, fuck, then when you, fuck, can't rearrange them then fuck, suddenly it's it's it's new information. suddenly it's yuck right? like i asked to be fucking saved. man didn't ask to be saved fam. i'm a real person you know not a woman-shaped hollow. what about dem dark bits. dem proper dark bits. dem invasive, protruding dark bits, that that that whatever the fuck they give me yeah and whatever the fuck i take yeah my eyelids are scalded fam – i see hell. and and so whenever whenever i fucking blink i'm. that dark. in

this dark place. yeah here. dem man dere? dem dark bits dere yeah? you can fuck with dem dark man dere yeah? look at dem, deya all around us. cameras for eyes, a pound coin for a heart. dem man got stamina. dem man carry blades under their tongues. relentless my g. hardcore niggas. my you… love my honesty mike? my my fucked-up ways, angry at the worldisims. soldier body. whore mouth. [i'm just] skin and concept. and then body. distant. fiery… lost… ah ah. no. no

cahi'm smart man… like my mother was this library and i can't read a page. i'm fucking. and and i find myself talking. i hear words coming from. and insides. and they say ask for help and i ask for help but it always goes. and chalky white and pinks. and meetings. and the strategies. it's like if you need a strategy for something; then you struggle with it man. and the morning punches you in the gut, strangling you and stabbing at the sides of your face. and faces. and my shadow sits at the end of my bed gnawing at my toes, using my scabs as toothpicks and my shame as their breakfast. ah you dat? you want all that ? take my knickers.

MICHAEL. –

ESHE. take them

ESHE *lies on her back and takes off her knickers.*
She slides them down her crutch.
Stands on the bed and waves them in his face.

MICHAEL. –

ESHE. take them michael

MICHAEL. –

MICHAEL *takes the knickers from the end of the crutch.*
He takes her crutch from her and puts it down.

He walks away from her.
He makes himself a large drink.
ESHE *stands on her bed.* ESHE *can see what she says next.*

issa full moon tonight you like looking at the moon

ESHE. i was watching *planet earth* and this lioness. she was gorgeous. strong back great eyes and she had her cubs with her; four or five of them. the father of her cubs had been slaughtered, so this lioness was hunting, protecting and providing all by herself. anyway, one night she goes out hunting for food as usual, and leaves her cubs sleeping – as usual. she hears predators coming for her babies… so she roars right, so that they are threatened and run away. the predators i mean. we see her realise it. she hasn't heard that her babies are safe. peak. she panics. she's running back. we see her. and it's too late. her babies are gone. her flesh. her world. there's no mess, no blood – just empty home. space. she lets out this roar mike, this painful, deep, like from the pit of… achy. real.

and then she's up. bang. and she searches the whole night. stamina. and then night turns into the next day – she is still looking. day into a few days – into a few weeks. they zoom in on her and she's.

…sort of. kind of a shape that used to resemble her. she's stopped looking after herself. she's not eating. and so she just stops. in the middle of the jungle… this tiny… and… familiar… and she lays down and dies.

ESHE *feels sick and runs to the bathroom.*
MICHAEL *takes in the room.*
He finds a bottle of brandy.
And then a bottle of white rum.
He drinks some.
He pours the rum down the drain.
He fills the rum with water.
He leaves the brandy.
He goes to fill them with water.
MICHAEL *finds more bottles.*
He puts them in the bin.
He looks in her drawers to find some clean bed sheets.
He knows where they are.
He starts to clean up.

MICHAEL. music. music

MICHAEL *is looking for a specific vinyl.*
MICHAEL *is looking for a vinyl player.*

He finds the box marked 'God Days'.
He finds a picture of ESHE *and her mother and places it on her bedside.*
He finds the vinyl he was looking for. He hears the broken vinyl pieces. He looks inside the vinyl case.
It's difficult for him.
He looks under her pillows and he finds her phone.
He can't enter it.
And a letter addressed to ELLA.
He unfolds the letter and begins to read.
He hears the toilet flush and folds it back and puts it in his waistband.
ESHE *returns.*

can i stay here tonight?

ESHE. nah i'm good b

MICHAEL. i want to stay for me

ESHE. for you?

MICHAEL. yeah… yes

ESHE. didn't ask

MICHAEL. wanted to help

ESHE. –

MICHAEL. is that your mum's 'good day' box?

ESHE. michael when did you get here? nice to see you

ESHE *makes a drink.*

MICHAEL. been here for a minute eshe

ESHE. seen. stop shouting at me

MICHAEL. –

ESHE *takes off her socks*

they are wet

glitter

ESHE *floats.*

who do you need me to call?

ESHE *sings the first line of Prince's 'Purple Rain'.*

let's play a song. rest your voice

ESHE *sings the second line of Prince's 'Purple Rain'.*
MICHAEL *sings the next line.*
ESHE *and* MICHAEL *sing the following line together.*

why did ella break the vinyl

ESHE. charge your phone?

MICHAEL. i'd give you my blood, clothes off my back if you needed

ESHE. –

MICHAEL. why don't you want me eshe?

ESHE *starts drawing.*

i just wanted to be 'a' reason not 'the' reason. i love you front to back, sped up and in slow motion. always have. your mum knew. my mum asks about you every day man. forgets her own name, forgets where she lives half the time now. she always, every night asks if i've. she thinks that we're still – and i'm just lying to her.

…i'm sorry that i did this to you. i'm sorry i was driving and i'm sorry that i didn't remind you to buckle up okay? just wanted to get you home, safe. ella was belling and. look… i will stay here with you even if you don't want me to. you're tryna push me away but i'm here i don't want you any other way. just alive. happy. free.

ESHE. and yours. free and yours… i don't love you. the door's open.

MICHAEL. i can't watch this

ESHE. oh?

MICHAEL. i have limits

ESHE. mister save-a-hoe patterson does not have limits. i don't care about the fucking accident. i wished you hit a pole and i wished it plunged through my brain and into my ancestry

MICHAEL. you're drunk

ESHE. yes. and you stand for nothing

MICHAEL. off your face

ESHE. insightful classes too. well done

MICHAEL. what have you taken?

ESHE. reality. i've taken reality

ESHE *gets up and stumbles.*
MICHAEL *offers his hand.*
ESHE.
ESHE *brings out a whole bottle of unopened brandy.*
ESHE *drinks from the bottle.*
There is a scuffle between them as MICHAEL *attempts to stop* ESHE *from drinking the whole thing.*
She is very strong.
It's surprising for MICHAEL.
She bites his hand.
ESHE *gets her crutch and forces the crutch between her and* MICHAEL.
She drinks the whole bottle.
As she does, MICHAEL *tries to get to her but she means it.*
MICHAEL *watches her.*

ESHE *begins to cry.*
MICHAEL *begins to cry.*

i just want my mum.

MICHAEL. i'm gonna call the hospital eshe, i don't know what you've taken but i've seen how much you've drank and. were gonna get you a black woman doctor yeah. no waiting list. no white people not believing you. no misconduct of any kind. we're going to go now. because i don't know what you need.

ESHE. when sea otters sleep they hold their loved ones in their hands

MICHAEL. here.

ESHE. too late

MICHAEL. never

ESHE. i wanna hold your hand inside you. i wanna love like i've never known violence

MICHAEL. you can

ESHE. where. where

MICHAEL *brings a rose to* ESHE.

atlantis?

MICHAEL. yeah, atlantis

ESHE. roses have auras.

MICHAEL. seen.

ESHE. trees get to have summer and winter

ESHE *happily surrenders to her own winter.*

MICHAEL. yeah they do. it's nice. just gonna pack a bag, where's your meds?

ESHE.…

MICHAEL. where's your meds eshe?

The letter with ELLA*'s name on it is visible.*
MICHAEL *calls* ELLA.

why didn't you tell me she was this bad. what? we gotta take her somewhere. what? i'm not arguing with you again. you tire me man. she's asking for you. yeah. yeah in a bit.

MICHAEL *takes off his shirt.*
ESHE *is in her ocean.*
MICHAEL *plays a vinyl – 'Sweet Love' by Anita Baker or something of that ilk is fitting here.*

He walks over to ESHE *and sits with her.*
She rejects him.
He insists.
She places her face on his chest.
He kisses her forehead.
He whispers something in her ear.
She signal to the bathroom.

He goes to the bathroom.
ESHE*'s mermaid tail glistening.*
ESHE *tries to sing along to the vinyl.*
ESHE *has lost her voice.*
ESHE *rolls under the bed.*
MICHAEL *comes out with some baby wipes.*
He wipes ESHE*'s face.*
He wipes her neck.
He wipes her armpit.
He wipes her mouth.
MICHAEL *kisses* ESHE *on the mouth.*

ELLA. michael? michael

MICHAEL (*to himself*). did she fly here?

ELLA. michael!

MICHAEL. fuck

ELLA. hello. michael. eshe.

MICHAEL.…

ELLA. hello michael. michael

MICHAEL. –

ELLA. michael! eshe.

MICHAEL. yes man. yeah. yeah okay i'm coming. don't you have a key?

ELLA. i'm respecting boundaries.

MICHAEL. –

ELLA. jesus christ michael open the door

MICHAEL *opens the door for* ELLA, *it's not easy.*
ELLA *goes to walk in but is stopped by* MICHAEL*'s presence – he is topless.*
She collects herself
and pushes past him.

MICHAEL.…

ELLA.…

MICHAEL. ...

ELLA. where is she

MICHAEL. –

ELLA. where is she mike

MICHAEL. –

ELLA. where the fuck is my girlfriend

MICHAEL. how you get here so quick

ELLA. what has happened in here?

MICHAEL. was you just waiting around

ELLA. no

MICHAEL. waiting on your little bike with your little helmet. where'd you go?

ELLA. –

MICHAEL *attends* ESHE.
ELLA *takes in the room.*
ELLA *opens the vinyl slip and realises* ESHE *has broken it.*
ELLA *makes the decision to join them.*
ESHE *turns her face to* ELLA.
ELLA *strokes her face and kisses her forehead.*
MICHAEL *puts his arm around* ESHE.
ELLA *does the same.*
ESHE *tries to hold* ELLA*'s hand.*
ELLA *gets up.*
She puts the roses in water.

MICHAEL. what you doing?

ELLA *starts to clean.*

what are you do/ing ella

ELLA. i'm staying. helping

MICHAEL. she's under the bed

ELLA. washing up

MICHAEL. she's under the fucking bed

ELLA. i can see that.

MICHAEL. and?

MICHAEL *drinks some brandy.*

hello? earth to robot. hello

MICHAEL *starts packing a bag.*

i dunno what she sees in you

ELLA. –

MICHAEL. i'm talking to myself?

ELLA. –

MICHAEL. she's under the fucking / bed!

ELLA. just pack a fucking bag michael, for fuck's sake

MICHAEL. what

ELLA. washing up.

MICHAEL. what?

ELLA. that's the task that i am doing.

MICHAEL. what? you begged me to answer the door and you're standing there washing mugs

ELLA. i'm respecting boundaries. and i'm and trying to start / the process of getting things back to normal for her

MICHAEL. my car is outside it's nearly dawn man. who do we call?

ELLA. –

MICHAEL. i swear to god

ELLA. i'm gonna finish up here. and then were going to arrange a cab to come and take us to a&e calmly and quietly.

MICHAEL. fuck you ella

ELLA. you already tried

MICHAEL. seen. it was a kiss and man was drunk

ELLA. it was inappropriate

MICHAEL. are you a sociopath. are you capable of anything other than that? this? micromanaging and patrolling

MICHAEL *grabs* ELLA *and forces her to look at* ESHE.

ELLA. don't grab me, i'm not your mate. don't touch me

MICHAEL. nothing nah?

ELLA. don't touch me

MICHAEL. fuck this

MICHAEL *picks* ESHE *up in his arms.*
Proudly.
Pathetically.
Definitely.
He displays her body.
He displays his physical strength.
Maybe he holds her above his head to ELLA.
Displaying the woman he loves most, to the woman he hates most.

ELLA. don't you fucking touch / her

MICHAEL. what are you doing for / her

ELLA. put her down!

MICHAEL. what have you done for her? /

ELLA. put her down are you insane

MICHAEL. what have you been doing to her?

ELLA. what are you doing, what are you showing?

MICHAEL. what are *you* doing ella… fuck. do something! / call someone

ELLA. i am doing / things…

MICHAEL. you called me to come / over

ELLA. i shouldn't have

MICHAEL. but you did. you did cos you know she needs us both and you fucking hate it.

MICHAEL *puts* ESHE *down.*

ELLA. i think your fucking stupid face on your face /

MICHAEL. this is time-consuming /

ELLA. what have you done that's been helpful? enable and 'yes' everything? hmmm? placate? scream, and sing and smoke yourselves to, drink yourselves to. look at the place!

MICHAEL. you let it get like this. this [is] / your gaff

ELLA. tell me! tell me what it is that you've done tonight? hold her really really close as you reminisce about the good times about bird's-eye meals and bird's-eye dreams and /

MICHAEL. bird's-eye is crazy

ELLA. or did you bond over your dead –

MICHAEL. …finish that sentence. i want her to hear you finish that.

He squares up to ELLA.
She squares him right back.

you left her you heartless bitch

you saw all of this. and you left.

ELLA. she didn't want me here

MICHAEL. she doesn't want me here.

ELLA. –

MICHAEL. she never wants me around any more. but that's what you wanted. her all to yourself. succubus. no feeling

ELLA. i have feelings.

Beat.
ELLA *has a coughing fit.*
MICHAEL *watches.*

what's she taken. i need to know what she has taken so i can inform the next steps to her team

MICHAEL. i know this

ELLA. do you know? do you know that she's really unwell at the moment actually

MICHAEL. she drank maybe a litre of brandy and been popping two two naproxen. who do we call and how do we get there?

ELLA. you drove her home pissed, now look at her. i know exactly what pain medication she's prescribed and why

MICHAEL. i don't need your forgiveness ella

ELLA. you don't have it. everyone thinks it's simple. it's not simple… they're just gonna send her back here. even if they section her / she will

MICHAEL. she can hear you /

ELLA. even if she gets overnight care, they will just send her back here. we've done this dance michael

MICHAEL. you chose her. and this.

ELLA. what? you don't know what i chose. my choices are absolutely none of your concern excuse me.

MICHAEL. she is. her. she is the choice you made. as a whole, a whole human. and you chose to stay

ELLA. i know what i chose at the time michael

MICHAEL. choose her now. fucking choose her

ELLA. i am. and myself. just give me a second / to

MICHAEL. nah you don't get a second you've had plenty

ELLA. and you hate it. you lost.

MICHAEL. –

ELLA. you've been around for more than a decade. and you lost her to me.

MICHAEL. she's not a prize

ELLA. a whole penis and bulging biceps and you lost her to me

MICHAEL. i'm not competing

ELLA. you're not a competitor

MICHAEL. she's not a trophy

ELLA. why is your shirt off?

A pause.

MICHAEL. she needs to feel love right now. she needs to know that she is safe but what she's doing is unsafe

ELLA. did you read that in a book?

MICHAEL. fuck you ella

ELLA. google?

MICHAEL. prick

ELLA. you think you can love her back to health? love her back to happiness? you loved her into the arms of a woman so now what?

ELLA *has a coughing fit.*

ELLA *drinks some water.*

ESHE*'s alarm clock that she set earlier becomes more apparent.*
ESHE *hears her alarm clock.*

MICHAEL. she doesn't like taking pills and going there

ELLA. it's not about what she likes. it's about keeping her alive

MICHAEL. who do we call ella?

ELLA. she's not going to remember any of this… pointless noise

MICHAEL *retreats.*
ESHE *holds her alarm clock.*
ELLA *washes up.*

MICHAEL. i love every fucking hair on her head. she's lying there… lean. lean ella… she's tiny. like. i get it, you've seen this all before yeah, it's even boring to you; bit too loud i get it yeah. cool, well done. thank you. nobody can look after her like you can. mvp. champion. champion.

Beat.

can you please tell me who to call so she can be seen?

ELLA *washes up.*
ESHE *is in Atlantis.*

it's the control innit? you're unqualified to love so you seek out those that crave it, you feed. so you can feel alive whilst being dead. some emotional tourist. a coward. parasite.

ELLA *brings a mirror to* MICHAEL.
She holds it in his face.
MICHAEL *takes the mirror.*
ELLA *dials a number.*

ELLA. hello, yeah i'm making a crisis call on behalf on of somebody i know… eshe bird, second of november 1989… yeah… she's intoxicated, conscious and currently going through an episode… manic depressive, yeah. yes the same address… she recently split from somebody, her girlfriend… yes… the same address yes… correct yes… mm-hm… yes that's fine i'll stay on the line… thanks

MICHAEL *tends to* ESHE.
MICHAEL *packs a bag.*
ELLA *watches* MICHAEL, *letter addressed to* ELLA *in his waistband.*
ESHE *is transforming.*
Maybe she changes her wig, or hat. Maybe she gets new skin. She is in ecstasy.

is that my name

MICHAEL. what?

ELLA *opens the letter.*
ELLA *reads it.*
ELLA *gasps.*

ella?

ELLA. she planned an overdose

MICHAEL. what?

ELLA *drops her phone; alarm clock goes off.*

ESHE *is a mermaid.*

ESHE *is swimming in her ocean*

red lights

blue lights

sirens

waterfalls

glitter

tick tock

water

waves

crashing

blue

Floaty *beeping.*

Panic.

Hospital sounds.

Pumping.

floaty

swim

baby crying

Tears.

screaming

PARAMEDIC VOICE. i need you to work together to help eshe.

SISSY VOICE

rain

glitter

End of Act One.

ACT TWO

…the hospital

The following evening.
'God Day' box is next to ESHE.
ESHE *is in a hospital bed, sleeping.*
ELLA *is by* ESHE*'s side.*
MICHAEL *is by* ESHE*'s side.*
In sleep, ESHE *tosses and turns.*
ELLA *holds* ESHE*'s hand.*

ELLA (*to* ESHE). oh darling it's okay. it's okay. you're not alone eshe. you're surrounded by such love. and guess what? can you keep a secret? there's the most bubbliest, foamiest, warmest bath in all of bethnal green just waiting for you to enter it. every time you relax my love, every time you're sleeping peacefully an ancestor does the same. beautiful girl. with beautiful dreams and a beautiful brain; everything will be beautiful. i promise.

MICHAEL. why'd you lie to her like that?

ELLA. i'm not lying

MICHAEL. seen. you believe what you're saying?

ELLA. yes.

MICHAEL. can you do all that? make it pretty and perfect or what/ever

ELLA. can you? do you? do you even want beautiful things for her?

MICHAEL. course i do. but telling her things she won't get to see. telling her stuff that ain't realistic / or true

ELLA. says who? you? what do you know about the promises i've made to her? i know that you've seen things and experienced events together and timelines that i will never know. i respect that.

MICHAEL.…

ELLA. but she is the most beautiful creature i've ever seen and the most beautiful creature that's ever seen me back. she looks at me like the sun lives in my chest. and i don't consent to wishing or wanting darkness for her.

MICHAEL.…you think i do?

ELLA. why didn't you read the letter?

MICHAEL. i did

ELLA. you didn't think to call an ambulance or

MICHAEL. she didn't know i was reading it

ELLA. –

MICHAEL. she was in the toilet. found it when she was throwing up. opened it, heard her coming back. i just panicked and stopped

ELLA. panicked?

MICHAEL. she don't like when people go through her stuff

ELLA. you did anyway

MICHAEL. aren't you grateful that i did?

ELLA. how can you have read that and not continued in grave grave concern?

MICHAEL. how could you have seen her, and left?

ELLA. i was just at the end of the road. i wasn't far. i didn't leave. i was doing right by her by respecting her wishes and by waiting.

MICHAEL. in the cold outside?

ELLA. i could have gone to my parents'

MICHAEL. why didn't you? where it's warm. what you running from?

ELLA.…

MICHAEL. cos if she's what you're running into, that ain't fair

ELLA. why was your shirt off when i came michael?

MICHAEL. was hot. just read the letter and

ELLA. didn't call an ambulance

MICHAEL. she talks like that, been talking like that. she writes how she talks. so when i read the letter. it's. she's always spoke like that / so i didn't see

ELLA. what does that mean michael.

MICHAEL. that she feels a lot. like all the time. big and nuff, and a lot. equals eshe. i'm saying stuff to you that you already know. no?

ELLA. …

MICHAEL. –

ELLA. i think she hides it from me

MICHAEL. what

ELLA. …

MICHAEL. what?

ELLA. she doesn't sing when i'm around. i never get to hear her. or read her poetry. or see her art.

MICHAEL. i'm sure she wants to show it to you ella. that side of her.

ELLA. …

MICHAEL. are you done with her? dunno man you queer lot and your on and off again.

ELLA. i don't know

MICHAEL. she came over that night cos i asked her to. it's weird like grieving someone you've never met. grieving someone you never knew

ELLA. she told me about your dad the other day i didn't know.

MICHAEL. and i told her not to.

ELLA. sorry about what i said before

MICHAEL. nothing you say affects me ella.

ELLA. okay

MICHAEL. i was mad at her for telling my business to people. it's my business. i handle me and mine. always have. always had to. so finding out this man, the man that gave my mum sperm, is six feet in the ground. dunno. the only one i knew, know in my life like. as an adult that has dealt with that. is her. you man still got both parents or even one. the grass is always greener i know. ain't saying your life is cushty cos you got family and that. but nothing prepares you for a parent dying. even if you hate that parent. nothing.

ELLA. sorry

MICHAEL. i'm telling you this for eshe. not me. i don't like you.

ELLA. i despise you

MICHAEL. you were blowing up her phone and she picked up to shut you up

ELLA. alright / alright

MICHAEL. your mouth is always moving though

ELLA. go on

MICHAEL. and you picked up and i was mouthing to her to not say where she was and why, cos you're tapped and want to own her and you flipped the last time me and her bucked up to go raving

ELLA. excuse me

MICHAEL. you are not excused. and every time you know she's with me, i mysteriously don't see her for months after. so yeah. hearing that that prick was dead – we got a bottle and. it was like old times man. i just wanted her around. i wanted her around for me. for as long as possible. without getting the green light from you. and i told her to lie to you. like i begged her to

ELLA. she's not a liar

MICHAEL. secretive though. that's what we fought about the night of the accident. its cos she was sad that i made her lie to you

ELLA. oh

MICHAEL. cos she loves you

ELLA. oh

MICHAEL. yeah

ELLA. she loves you too you know

MICHAEL. the letter was addressed to you. not me.

ESHE *starts to sing over* MICHAEL.

ESHE (*sarcasm*). blah blah blah blah blah blah
blee blee blee blee blee blee
bloo bloo bloo bloo bloo bloo
ha ha ha ha ha ha ha

wah wah wah
wah wha wah

how do i stay alive
love truly wants me to die
how do i stay afloat when
you keep crashing my boat
kiss my name
kiss my name
name a storm after me
i am game
kiss my name
kiss my name
name a storm after me
i'm insane

some of you want to own me
some of you want to share me
some of you wish you knew me
some of you wish you drew me

Humming and other harmonies can be heard.
ESHE*'s 'God Day' box glows.*

how do i stay alive
love truly wants me to die
how do i stay afloat
you keep fucking my boat

say my name
my full name
name a storm after me
i'm insane
let me be
i am free
it's your boxes that cut and suffocate me

i am this
i am that
i am none of it
i'm back

i cause devastation
i am devastation
i am divination
there's no destination
constant transformation

blah blah blah blah blah blah
blee blee blee blee blee blee
bloo bloo bloo bloo bloo bloo
ha ha ha ha ha ha ha

ESHE *is alive.*
Some of this is to ELLA.
Some of this is to MICHAEL.
Some of this is to us.
Some of this is to dem.

piercing drums, deafening hums, colliding sums of all
colours magnificent
a bellow of cries devour my skies, angels with knives, i bleed
black: maleficent
holding my breath, i'm poking with death, i soak up the wet,
dense, crystalised: meth.
dry swallow my dreams, choke on the seams, get cut on the
schemes, pay with extremes and man is still in debt

Some of the following loops.

in debt to the past
in debt to the first
in debt to the last
in debt to my thirst
the pink or the blue
the blue or the pink
the yellow the white
the blade or the knife

Jellyfish

saxophones

glitter

drums

bass

electric guitar

choral voice

time

we are now at ELLA*'s.*

my soil is dark
my soil is rich
my soul is half
my soul's a bitch
my soil is dark
my soil is rich
my soul is half
my soul's a bitch

i won't shut up
i can't shut up
my tongue is split
my tongue is rough
i can't be quiet
i want a riot
i won't be still
i can't be silent

you're looking at me, devouring me
studying me, wanting me yeah
copying me, learning from me, scared of me
but obsessed with me
you love me, you want me, you hate me, you draw me
the more me, i am me, the more me you hate me
i'm half of it i'm all of it, i'm none of it, i'm proud of it

the black of my eye
the black of my pain
the black of my nights
the black of my skies yeah
the black of my eye
the black of my pain
the black of my nights
are me on the rise

the black of my shadows
gospel in marrow
gospel in mothers
gospel in barrels

blah blah blah blah blah blah
blee blee blee blee blee blee
bloo bloo bloo bloo bloo bloo
ha ha ha ha ha ha ha

wah wah wah
wah wha wah
wah wha wha

SISSY VOICE. she's back

ELLA. morning love.

ESHE. huh?

ELLA. you were singing. in your sleep.

ESHE. sorry

ELLA. no no. i liked it. was nice to hear

ESHE. –

ELLA. you okay?

ESHE *nods.*

why don't you go back to sleep? been a long day.

ESHE. has it?

ELLA. yeah

ESHE. okay.

ELLA. i'm right here. whatever you want you just tap me okay my love

ESHE. 'kay

ESHE *goes back to sleep.*

ELLA. you wanna tell me about it?

ESHE. what

ELLA. your day

ESHE. oh

ELLA. i'm all ears

ESHE. didn't we just?

ELLA. here's your meds

ESHE. thanks

ELLA. okay. goodnight

ESHE. thank you

ELLA. i'm listening

ESHE. to what?

ELLA. to you

ESHE. okay

ELLA. goodnight

ELLA *sleeps.*

ESHE. huh

ELLA. good morning love

ESHE. yeah.

ELLA. sleep well?

ESHE. no

ELLA. i'm sorry

ESHE. what day is it

ELLA. are you crying

ESHE. am i?

ELLA. don't cry don't cry

ESHE. i'm not crying

ELLA. you can cry love if you need to

ESHE. i don't

ELLA. okay. here's your meds. sun's out today we can go for a walking meditation

ELLA *hands* ESHE *some medicine.*

ESHE. thank you

ELLA. ready for *the l-word*?

ESHE. season two

ELLA. obviously. you're doing really well esh. doing all your steps. i'm so proud of you

ELLA *gets in bed with* ESHE.
ELLA *puts her arm around* ESHE.
It feels. New.
They remain in an embrace.

ESHE *sleeps.*

ELLA *drinks.*
ELLA *smokes.*

ESHE *sleeps.*

perfect. your hair looks lovely

ESHE. huh?

ELLA. you look great. you suit any style

ESHE. the days are rolling into one

ELLA. it's okay

ESHE. i know it's okay. you don't have to agree with everything i say. that's not what i meant when i said i wanted to be free.

ELLA. are you okay

ESHE. i've got a headache

ELLA. that's okay. and i'm sorry to hear; here's some water

ESHE. thank you

ELLA. wanna hear a joke?

ESHE. sure

ELLA. why don't jellyfish make good secret agents?

ESHE. ella

ELLA. no no it's a good one

ESHE. i don't know why jellyfish don't make good secret agents please tell me

ELLA. because they are always being transparent!

ESHE. god

ELLA. no wait it's because they're too transparent

ESHE. headache

ELLA. oh sorry. hopefully the pills kick in soon. why don't you nap?

ESHE. yeah

ELLA. when you wake we can go for a nice walk? look at some trees

ESHE *sleeps.*

ELLA *watches* ESHE *sleep.* ESHE *seems to be having a hard night sleeping.*

ELLA *sings a longing song to* ESHE. *Maybe Joan Armatrading's 'The Weakness in Me' or something of that ilk.*

i miss you

ESHE. i'm right here.

ELLA. you're back?

ESHE. never left.

ELLA *kisses* ESHE *on the mouth.*
ESHE *kisses her back.*

End of Act Two.

ACT THREE

ELLA*'s house.*

ESHE *is up.*
She smokes.
ESHE *watches* ELLA *sleep.*
ESHE *silently screams.*
She collects herself.
ESHE *gets out of bed.*

ELLA. she's up.

ESHE. didn't mean to wake you

ELLA. up and at it

ESHE. small small

ELLA. rising and shining

ESHE. early bird, worm and that

ELLA. i was thinking

ESHE. when

ELLA. what

ESHE. if you were asleep, when were you thinking?

ELLA. for a while. when i'm up silly. i think when i'm up

ESHE. right

ELLA. i was thinking it's been over a month since you were in mental prison and i was thinking just a bit, not too much haha. that we go do something really really lush. like celebrating you. celebrate us. paint the town red. doll ourselves up. you're doing all the steps. we are doing all the steps and i just. i'm so

ESHE. proud of me. you say it every day

ELLA. it's cos i mean it. i was thinking maybe we could chat about us. again

ESHE. i just woke up el

ELLA. of course. it's just an idea... we can make it a tab and we can go back to it. what do you think? no rush darling. no rush. my mum sends her love again and my dad says 'speedy recovery'. they sent you a 'self-care' hamper. nice right? i'd rather they just sent the money though. but hey. money. rent. yes. your agent got in touch about starting up meetings again.

ESHE. –

ELLA. you left your laptop open

ESHE. going through my emails?

ELLA. no no. your laptop was making lots of noise. i just wanted it to stop. the noise. notifications. the flashing.

ESHE. right

ELLA. yeah. so nice to see you like this. i love it when you're like this. when we're like this.

ESHE. same

ELLA *goes to the toilet.*
There is a knock at the door.

MICHAEL. she's up.

ESHE. huh?

MICHAEL. didn't mean to wake you

ESHE. wake me?

MICHAEL. rising and shining

ESHE. early bird, worm and that

MICHAEL. i was thinking

ESHE. huh when

MICHAEL. what

ESHE. if you were asleep, when were you thinking?

MICHAEL. i'm up silly. i think when i'm up

ESHE. right

MICHAEL. i was thinking it's been over a month since you were in mental prison and i was thinking we go do something like we go margate or something. pebble beach. you like stones and that. the water. i made you this from the last time we went. here. i'm so proud /

ESHE. proud of me. you say it every day

MICHAEL. you alright?

ESHE. yeah

MICHAEL. come here

MICHAEL *opens his arms wide and* ESHE *runs into them. A small kiss happens.*

SISSY VOICE. this bit don't last

ELLA. hey hey

ESHE *and* MICHAEL *stop.*

packed your car. we ready?

ESHE. where we going

ELLA. to the beach

ESHE. what?

MICHAEL. last week you said you wanted to go back again

ESHE. again?

ELLA. to celebrate your eight weeks of being home

MICHAEL. back at ella's

ELLA. home

ESHE. yes. i'm just. eight weeks? two months?

MICHAEL. yeah

ELLA. yeah

ESHE. but you just said a month ago?

MICHAEL. mad woman when?

ESHE. okay. now

MICHAEL. you alright esh

ELLA. you feeling okay eshe?

SISSY VOICE. how you keeping long time

ESHE. yeah just gonna shower

ELLA. great.

MICHAEL (*to* ELLA). you look [so awful]… you look ella

ELLA. you look [awful like you always do] michael too michael

ESHE *exits.*

she's doing really good you know.

MICHAEL. yeah. she's doing really good.

ELLA. –

MICHAEL. –

ELLA. –

MICHAEL.…

ELLA.…

MICHAEL.…

ELLA. you look like shit

MICHAEL. you look like death

ELLA. she's what matters though.

MICHAEL. she's what matters though

ELLA. she's what matters though

MICHAEL. she's what matters though

ELLA. she's what matters though

MICHAEL. she's what matters though

ELLA. she's what matters though

MICHAEL. she's what matters though

ELLA. she's what matters though

MICHAEL. she's what matters though

ELLA. she's what matters though

SISSY VOICE. blah blah blah blah bloo bloo bloo bleeeeeeeee

ESHE *comes out of the bathroom.*

MICHAEL. she's what matters though

ELLA. she's what matters though

MICHAEL. she's what matters though

ELLA. she's what matters though

SISSY VOICE. can't reach dem. they can't reach you.

ESHE *looks at us.*
ESHE*'s boat appears. And she sits in it.*
Her tail is tied up.

ESHE. you guys can go as well.

ESHE *goes to sit in her boat.*
Maybe they get into her boat with her.
She tries to get her boat to move.

SISSY VOICE. won't ever reach you

She accepts she can't.

ESHE. don't cry. it's okay: jellyfish glow in the dark.

End of play.

Extracts from Eshe's Diary

November 2015

Dvsdofjdsgovsfg;jdf;ogjsfokglskgvsk;gvsgsl'kdfkdgzjo;doj;
bfjvsjvbsjkvjklvsjkvsfj;vjdo;fj;fsjh;osfguirshrigvurshgvousrh
jgoierjgp'ierjsd'pgijerg;oisrjhg'v`srhjigvz;rsoghjvzslryh;`ghjv
ior;wgt8uwruqyahwdhbcknnd v.,dfnbh;prtjhrso`f;hbd

December 2st 2015

Shes gone.

December 14th 2015

What is a good poem

How do we know if a poem is good
On a tuesday evening i dont know what to do with my rage

4.5 out of seven is my week
My pronouns are he him
I nearly got mercury poisoning
This is my first time
And I am tired
On tuesdays evenings my rage over takes
What is the difference between the full and new moon
I am an interlude
Happy wednesday
My body is bouncing back into spring
I am feeling a little bit powerful
A little bit
Bits

I am lots of bits

In pressure. Under pressure
Always under
Alot of day dreaming
I dream when im awake
It was very difficult to find my new therapist
Whose g0oing to drink the most rum?
Going from thing to thing
I have to get a suit

And write a speech
Were broke until then
Im in the sun with my cat until then
Hopefully il have a job by then
Not having a job is stressful
Having a job is stressful

When we are not thinking about translating and being smart is a good poem
The most beautiful poem in the world has already been written because you are born
This is a crap poem. I think i perform my gender.

January 2nd

I just googled that a white man has installed a solar powered radio thing that plays toto's africa in the namibian desert twenty four hours a day. Seven days a week. and its made me want to never google anything again. Happy new year.

January 15th

I don't understand why people take on jobs with crazies if they hate crazies? Isn't that tapped? It's like teachers don't wanna accept they are agents of state violence and security guards are failed police officers. You're working with vulnerable people in order to what? Contain and control? Fucking tapped. She doesn't even look me in the eyes. How am i gonna open up to you if you can't find my eyes. How am i gona not feel gross, or expel my gross if i cant find your fucking eyes man. I don't want this in me. I'd also like to not be this person too amy.

You're not the only one who hates me. Only thing separating crazies and you are headphones eshe. Remember that. I think my breasts have stopped growing. I think want them smaller. Or off.

May

trying my best to make sense connections of disconnections and i'm running out of spaces to go. Maybe im a garden. Or an eco system. Ecosystems are respected right?

Was reading up about Black pessimism, Black pain is not a narrative because it doesnt end. My intersections of pain arent 'milestones' or 'barriers to overcome' because Black pain is not a narrative. fuck.

june -

To start is to decide. Deciding where and how feels like a container. It feels as though to start is to manufacture a pool in the middle of a desert, when; before deciding to i was a liminal ocean with my own ecosystem. Where is the middle of an ocean? Where does an ocean start? If ocean evaporates sometimes and changes tides sometimes where does ocean start and end? I have been thinking of formless things non contained things. And i think of my memories and how they are so contained. Containers actually. See through, chinese take away crappy ill fitted lid type container. Plastic. Contained. Four sides. Most importantly; a lid. My memories feel like stacks of containers, i go to the cupboard and there they are, stacked, dusty and not ordered theres no labels and i cant see really from the outside whats inside. And when i open one, i think its a meal from last week but it might be one from last year. And the smell, i open the memory container and the smell is as potent as it was when i shoved it into a box of plastic. Actually the plastic boxes themselves are adding to a stale stench. And this cupboard is slowly making itself known to me.

I think i live in a black box. And inside this box is darkness. Complete black. What fills it, is me. This formless soul inside a body that sometimes does match the description of it. Maybe not a box, i think its a room, i think i live in an opaque black room and outside this room is the sun. brightness. And ive been waking up in that room, sleeping in that room, eating in that room, praying in that room, lying in that room, and sometimes someone comes along and i'm like oh yeah, light. Light does exist and oh yeah light doesn't run out. And oh yeah light moves. Light is something that can exist in a person and it can travel. And then the light leaves the room. And I'm back in pitch black. And then i get so confused because i've tasted and i've seen and i know that light exists. And so i run out. I run to the door and I open it and I'm like here it is. See. let me just stay here. In it. Bask in it cos i know my beds in that dark room and my lifes in there. I grew up in that room and it's mine so actually at some point i have to go back. I can't sleep in the sun forever. There's no beds there. And so i go back. And the darkness surrounds and the occasional firefly comes in and we dance. And i wonder how the firefly get their wings.

I think michael has wings.

July

Dreams on psych wards and dem man

I dreamt of a family of pandas outside my garden. I woke up and vivian was there. And they had come to see me and it was a sunny day. We went out to the garden and there was this family of pandas. About four of them, beautiful black and white pandas. Eating this lush green food from my garden. Happy and silly. And i was in awe that they had come to see me. Stunned. And then I went closer to the garden and as I was about to open the door when the pandas turned into guerillas and became aggressive. And i became scared. They took over my garden and I couldn't go outside. I was scared for Vivian but also confused - where did the pandas go? Did i make out that i saw pandas? Why did they lie to me like that? Or did i just see what i wanted to? I realised that the garden door was slightly ajar and as i took a step to close it so they wouldnt come in - one of the gorillas came inside- they were quite cheeky- and they looked at me, like they knew me, like we had spoken before, like i had changed my form, like they had been waiting for me, like they were trying to recognise me or something. Like i had told them to meet me here, and then was angry with me because i was like late or changed, or of a language they could no longer understand. But they spoke to me with their eyes and I felt like they were asking me to take them away from the guerillas. They wanted me to choose them anyway. Even though they looked different to me, or to what i could understand, they held out their little hand and wanted me to take them with me and i was too scared. And the matriarch of the gorillas pulled them away from me and i ran out. And so now this family of gorillas is living in my living room and the baby is waiting for me to open the door.

August 2016

Our hands were the same size once

We werent allowed to sit at the dinner table with our hands showing
unless
they were holding cutlery

Or jesus

Sometimes you were cheeky. And you'd rest your elbows on the table top

Palms to cheeks when mum wasnt looking
You had this shine about you.
A sheen.
I remember wanting to protect it.
You.

I dont know how we had the same genes and i had no shine

But when i asked you *'how do you glow like that'*

You put your palm to mine and said *'here you go'*

I loved holding them when you took me out
Took me away
Took me Through.

Loved holding them in general because i bite my nails and you stopped doing that years ago so maybe the magic would rub off on me

I loved looking at you cos thats where i saw ‘me’

Loved looking at you because i thats where i saw them

Loved it when people looked at us together.
Nothing could ever contain you
I longed to fill a room the way you did

And i cant remember it exactly

I wish i could remember it exactly

But your hands
One day
Became beetroot
And

Soon after they
melted into bags

And i think they were really heavy
I think they were really full

Cos i couldn’t fit inside them anymore

And the door was locked

you fit into corners now

hunched over

religion-less

a wordless prayer

achingly Opaque

I sit on the bed trying to sew my own bags so we can share

Underneath the pillow you have left me a pair of gloves

With a note

'Wear these'

I never said thank you

January 2017

Transformation and change is the only constant. I think i want to kill my inner child because she wont grow up. What is gender? If kill 'her' what does that mean for my now? Will ella still love me if i kill 'her?' sometimes she looks at me like im odd. I feel like an odd thing in her arms. Maybe im odd? Ive never been looked at like im right. Michael looks at me like im everything. But im just me. Hell is empty because all the demons are here. Earth is ghetto. Sending my location. Just gotta find my space ship

A Nick Hern Book

... *blackbird hour* first published in Great Britain in 2025 as a paperback original by Nick Hern Books Limited, The Glasshouse, 49a Goldhawk Road, London W12 8QP, in association with Vital Xposure and the Bush Theatre, London

Cover design by Kieron (KieronLewis.com)

Designed and typeset by Nick Hern Books, London
Printed in the UK by Mimeo Ltd, Huntingdon, Cambridgeshire PE29 6XX

A CIP catalogue record for this book is available from the British Library

ISBN 978 1 83904 431 1

Woodland CARBON
www.woodlandcarbon.co.uk
NICK HERN BOOKS
Printed on Carbon Captured paper

www.nickhernbooks.co.uk/environmental-policy

Nick Hern Books' authorised representative in the EU is
Easy Access System Europe – Mustamäe tee 50, 10621 Tallinn, Estonia
email gpsr.requests@easproject.com